Unleashing the
Power of Two

Unleashing the Power of Two

A Strategic Approach to Strengthening Marriage

Wesley and Edrienne Brandon

www.unleashingthepoweroftwo.com

Library of Congress Control Number: 2010902677
ISBN: Hardcover   978-1-4500-5203-0
                  Softcover   978-1-4500-5202-3
                  Ebook   978-1-4500-5204-7

This book was printed in the United States of America.

To order additional copies of this book, contact:
Xlibris Corporation
1-888-795-4274
www.Xlibris.com
Orders@Xlibris.com
73301

Contents

Dedication

To our parents—Ed, Marta, Portia, and Wesley—for making us who we are today. Your love, example, and support continue to inspire us to tightly hold each other's hands and fearlessly reach as far we can see. A special thanks for giving birth to us thirteen days apart and sending us to Duke, where it all started.

Introduction

During our engagement, we made a decision to not only make our marriage our top priority, but to also build everything in our lives around our relationship. As two individuals, each with strong wills and high personal aspirations, we knew that this challenge would require purposeful planning and intentional design.

We believed it was our responsibility to deliberately create and live a life that would glorify the gift of marriage God gave us. So we did. We spent the first six months of our marriage applying to business school together, the next six months hoping for admission, and our first anniversary in a U-Haul heading for Harvard Business School to be classmates again. Since then, consistent with our marriage being our first priority, we have worked at the same company, and we have commuted to work together and have been each other's first-choice partner in playing golf together on the weekends.

Trust us—we are not saying that engaging in the same careers, activities, and interests is the reason for our success. We are also not saying that this is what we think you should do. We acknowledge that we take togetherness to another level, but that's not the source of our power. We designed a marriage based on principles and processes that allow our relationship to flourish and excel—something any couple that wants to unleash their marital bliss, potential, and power can do too.

Premise

There are five core principles that we have found that can unleash the full potential in a relationship. These principles have consistently brought power to our lives and the lives of many people we've worked with, counseled, and observed. These principles are also evident in powerful teams and organizations in business, politics, sports, and daily life.

We recognize that every relationship is different and made up of its own complex combination of personalities, challenges, and experiences. However, while the content and the context of each relationship are unique, we believe that these principles are applicable to a marriage at any stage, state, or tenure. By employing these principles, we believe you will take your relationship to a new level.

Principle 1

Get Grounded

We are fully aware and appreciative of what a blessing it is to be together. Our marriage is not only a testament to our commitment and devotion to each other, but also an even bigger testament and devotion to God.

Often, couples lose sight of the fact that their marriage is actually a form of worship. So many couples get married in a church, where they make a covenant with God and each other, and they move through the rest of their lives focused just on their commitment to each other. They forget that they took a solemn vow before God to love, cherish, and be a steward of the person they married.

Principle 2

Build a Vision Together

We create our future together.

The exercise of brainstorming, planning, and capturing our plans on paper has been a positive enabler in our relationship. We have found that words on paper strengthen good ideas and expose weak ones. They also create a level of accountability that every relationship needs.

Principle 3

Learn to be Powerful

As individuals and as a couple, we recognize that we are works in progress. Therefore, to stay together and stay strong, we have to continue to develop ourselves and grow.

If you want to improve and get better, you must first realize that there is room for growth; everything is not perfect. We are fortunate that we both share this belief and desire to get better and stronger not only as individuals, but also as a couple.

Principle 4

Execute for Excellence

Execution is everything. When we work together, we can accomplish anything.

One of the most rewarding aspects of our relationship has been the accomplishments we have been able to achieve together. No matter how strong or confident we may feel as individuals, we both know that our strength increases exponentially when we are together. We have been able to execute and achieve against our vision because we work effectively together.

Principle 5

Seek the Next Level

We constantly push and challenge each other to improve, get better, and move forward.

We are each other's biggest supporter and challenger. What else would you expect and want from the person who knows you better than anyone else? Since we know that we have each other's best interest at heart, we are comfortable accepting and giving pushes and pulls to help each other break new ground and grow in different dimensions in our lives.

We hope this book will help you unlock new discoveries, ignite healthy conversations, and fuel more power in yourself, your relationship with your partner, and your spirituality.

Get Grounded

Whatever is at the center of our life will be the source of our security, guidance, wisdom, and power.

—Stephen Covey

"With this ring, I thee wed. With all that I am and all that I have, I thee endow in sickness and in health, in poverty or in wealth, till death do us part. I honor you in the name of the Father, and of the Son, and of the Holy Spirit. Amen."

Sounds familiar? There was a time when the idea of spending the rest of your life with your partner was all you could think about. You couldn't wait until the day that you would pledge everything you have, everything you are, and everything you will ever be to them. Not only did you choose to do this, but you also chose to do this before God and everyone close to you. For many of us, reminiscing about this choice is a source of strength. In the midst of conflict and challenge, we may sometimes lose sight or have less enthusiasm about the choice and the pledge. However, strong couples keep that decision close and present in their minds, which helps them focus on the hopes and promises their relationship still has in store for them. Essentially, it awakens their awareness of their potential for power.

More important than a commitment to your partner, marriage is an unconditional commitment to God.

With our wedding vows, we pledged two very important things. First, we committed to spend the rest of our lives with another imperfect person. The imperfection of individuals is fundamental to why marriage can be challenging.

Since neither of us is perfect, it is a given that at some point, we will make mistakes that might upset, disappoint, or stress our partner. Imperfection also implies incompleteness, which means that, inevitably, we will both change. In light of this knowledge, we still made an unconditional commitment to spend the rest of our lives together as imperfect, conditional, subject-to-change people.

Secondly, we promised to meet each other's needs in a way that magnifies God. Fortunately, God is perfect and doesn't change. Therefore, by committing to God that we will take care of each other, we are making a covenant while standing on a perfect, unwavering, and unconditional foundation. Thank goodness; it is often challenging to maintain an unconditional commitment to meet the needs of a conditional person. When things get tough or don't go well, imperfection tempts us to lose sight of our commitment to care for each other and put each other first—no matter what. Imperfection makes us feel justified in our disdain or mistreatment of each other, leads us to make conditional decisions, and compels us to act in ways that do anything but honor God. That is why it is so important—especially during challenging times—to source the power, strength, and motivation that come from knowing that the covenant and responsibilities of marriage are bigger than just the two of you.

Commitment is a covenant.

Your commitment to God is of the utmost importance. This commitment afforded you the gift of marriage to your partner. Therefore, you must unconditionally honor your commitment to God by meeting your partner's needs.

God gave us marriage as a gift. At a minimum, be grateful to be given the choice to accept the gift of marriage.

God puts people and experiences in our lives to develop us and to teach us things He wants us to know. He gives us free will to choose how we accept, interact, and interpret these people and experiences. This choice we have is a big deal. It is often the difference between seeing things as just isolated, disconnected events or part of a larger, more divine plan. It is the difference between viewing a job loss as a setback or as one of many positive outcomes, such as an opportunity to learn from new people, a change of scenery, or removing you from a situation that may be, with or without your knowledge, detrimental to you.

It is easy to forget the gravity of how you and your partner got together in the first place. You asked and they said yes, or they asked and you said yes. True, God put them in your path, but you had a choice to ask them to be with you or a choice to say yes to them when they asked you to be with them. Out of everyone in the world—you. Not that other girl or that other guy—you.

Your marriage should be nurtured and taken care of just as you would take care of the other blessings God gave you. Since we are fully appreciative and aware of this gift, we make a point to spend time, in thought and action, developing our marriage and ourselves as partners, just as we would work to improve the other talents and gifts with which we have been blessed.

Being aware of the blessing of marriage is a common thread among the successful couples we have observed. They act on this awareness by being vocal in their appreciation for each other, demonstrating their gratitude by taking care of their partner, and ensuring that their actions always reflect positively on their marriage. Our advice? As often as you can, thank your partner. For what? Everything. Thank them for popping the question, or thank them for saying yes. Thank them for staying with you, putting up with you, coming home to you—as these are all choices.

Remind yourself every day why they caught your eye.

Inherent in that reminder is something that won't change and is still attractive to you. Let's be real; in the very beginning, there are fireworks—and sparks fly. Sparks can do one of two things: they can fizzle or ignite into a fire. In the relationships that convert from sparks to fire, the fire represents the energy, heat, and power that a loving partnership can bring. Over time, familiarity sets in and can test the attention span and interest level in a relationship. In other words, the fire might start to die down. Just like how external elements, such as moisture or lack of air, can threaten a fire, external pressure and factors can threaten the vitality of a marriage. Every relationship and every fire can be reignited and reenergized by the addition of more energy and more fuel—a consistent and deliberate renewal of your focus on the commitment you made.

When I met Wes, he was very unassuming. Not flashy—just humble, hardworking, and a good listener. With all the success that he has had, he still has those same qualities. He has all the reason in the world to be the opposite—and he just isn't. Early on in our courtship, he told me that he was attracted to powerful women and that power was a trait in me to which he was attracted. When I recall his comment, I am reminded that I am powerful. By revisiting these memories, I am reminded about what I love about him, what he loves about me, and how that person, although different in some ways, is still that same person in other ways.

Don't forget that you made a good choice.

A common thread among strong teams is that they do not allow themselves, as individuals or as a collective, to lose sight of the power and potential they have as a team. Similarly, strong couples acknowledge the strength of their union in words and actions to each other and to others around them. This practice inspires them to reinvest in their relationship as well as motivates them to persevere during the tough times. Thus, in challenging situations, they operate from a shared sense of confidence, in which they expect things to work out, versus a shared sense of uncertainty, in which they hope for things to work out.

When I met Edrienne, it did not take me long to realize that I had found someone special. In fact, I can remember having the conversation with one of my college buddies during our sophomore year that Ed was the one—that although we had just started dating, I could see myself marrying her. I had not seriously thought about marriage to any woman before Ed, but there was something about her that made it extremely clear to me that I would be lucky to share and spend the rest of my life with her. During that time in my life, two books from the Bible were especially comforting to me and served as a source of spiritual inspiration for me—Proverbs, which is focused on learning and wisdom, and Ecclesiastes, which is focused on the discovery of God's purpose for our lives. Both of these books would provide additional perspective and guidance to me as I laid the foundation for my professional plans and personal interests. Proverbs 18:22 reads, "A man who finds a wife finds a good thing and obtains favor from the Lord." Looking back, I was especially blessed to find someone so good for me so early in my life. If my life has been any indication of His promise, I can attest to the favor and richness that a strong partner can bring to your life. Marriage was designed to provide positive outcomes, and I was extremely committed to developing our relationship so it would be pleasing in the eyes of God.

Next to your relationship with God, your marriage takes priority over all the other commitments in your life.

Priority over all other commitments means over everything—your work, friends, extended family, and other extracurricular activities. This even means your children. We know that this notion might be rubbing some of you the wrong way. To put each other and your marriage first, you may need to reprioritize the amount of thought, time, and energy you give to your marriage versus your other commitments. The answers to these questions will help clarify your next steps:

- If my marriage is the number one priority in my life, how does it compare to my other commitments?
- Do I prioritize the needs of my partner over the needs of the rest of the people in my life, like my extended family, my boss, or my friends?

- Do I spend as much quality time bonding with my partner as I do my friends?

Now, the action required is simple but not necessarily easy. To get started, create an opportunity to talk to each other about your current priorities using examples of how you spend your time and your actions as a guide. If you spend more time with your friends than your partner on the weekend, try to adjust something, whether it's the activities you're doing or exchange your friends for your partner in the activity. We know this might feel like a compromise to some of you. Guess what? It absolutely is. Compromises should be considered enablers, not inhibitors, to a productive marriage.

One of our best examples of a healthy compromise is the role of golf in our weekends. Here's the logic: Wesley loves golf. Edrienne likes golf. Wesley and Edrienne love each other. So when Wes wants to play golf on the weekends, he always gives Edrienne the option to play golf with him first before he asks his friends. That way, Edrienne always knows that Wesley is prioritizing spending time with her and that she has the option to decline or ask him to schedule golf around something she may have planned for them or herself. This way, they both feel accommodated, and everyone wins. This will result in making some tough choices and what may feel like sacrifices. To achieve a certain level of success in any aspect of your life that is important to you requires tough choices. Think of anyone that you admire for achieving a high level of success, and we guarantee that they made some sacrifices to get there. Some couples succeed by gradually folding these changes into their lives, and others do better by going cold turkey. Try and see what works for you. Remember, one big change can sometimes be just as liberating as ten small changes.

The Bottom Line

- Cherish your marriage since it is a gift from God.
- Be grateful to be given the choice to be in a relationship as rewarding as a marriage.
- Remind yourself as often as possible that you made a good choice and why you made that choice.
- Prioritize your marriage above all else.

Build a Vision Together

> Far better it is to dare mighty things, to win glorious triumphs even though checkered by failure, than to rank with those timid spirits who neither enjoy nor suffer much because they live in the gray twilight that knows neither victory nor defeat.
>
> —Theodore Roosevelt

One of the things that we love dearly about Harvard Business School is its mission to educate leaders who make a difference in the world. While a mission is focused on your purpose and how you plan to achieve that purpose, a vision is broader, future focused, and centered on what you want to be. One of the most important things a leader can do is set a vision. Leaders also energize others and enable them to achieve results. For a relationship to be as powerful and rewarding as possible, both partners must be engaged in setting a vision for what they want their relationship to be and keep each other motivated to achieve that vision so they can reap and enjoy the rewards of their success. Through a process that consists of a series of healthy discussions followed by some formal decisions about your plan for the future, you can work together to achieve this vision. In the business world, we call this process strategic planning, which is a fancy term for a well-thought-out plan written on paper in advance. Given our shared backgrounds in business, we have found the utilization of strategic planning in our own marriage has propelled our ability to successfully achieve the vision we have for our lives.

Two visions are not better than one.

Building your vision starts with understanding what you and your partner want in life. These are questions that can help bring your ambitions and preferences alive, being mindful and sensitive to what each person considers negotiable and nonnegotiable:

- What do we want to accomplish together? Individually?
- What are our priorities together? Individually?
- How do we want to live? Where do we want to live?
- What do our career paths look like? How does that influence our personal lives?

Another key input into the process of developing your vision is completing an honest assessment about your strengths and weaknesses as individuals. This will help you create a healthy interdependence in which you leverage your strengths and feel valued.

These efforts will enable you to clarify and understand what each other expects out of life and what capabilities you are bringing to the partnership. Then the objective becomes agreeing on a set of expectations that adds up to a vision that is attractive to both of you. As a rule of thumb, we think a good vision starts with "To be." Some say it's a one-sentence statement. It can be. However, the most important thing is to paint a picture with your words of what you want your ideal life to be.

Let's meet three couples—the Millers, the Carters, and the Fosters—and see the vision they have set for their lives:

Couple	Vision Statement
The Millers	**To reach the pinnacle of success in our professional lives without distraction.** We don't want to have a big family. In fact, we don't want to have kids at all. We just want to focus on us, our careers, and our freedom. We want to live downtown where the action is.
The Carters	**To be the best parents to as many children as possible.** It is extremely important for us to have a big family. While one of us will work in the home to raise our children, the other will work outside the home and provide income to support our livelihood. Space is important to us, so we would like a big house in a kid-friendly community with plenty of places for our kids to play.
The Fosters	**To contribute to society through a life devoted to public service.** One of us wants to run for public office, so we need to live in a certain location and stay there so we can develop roots and meet the right people. We need to get involved in the community and place ourselves very much in the public eye.

Expectations cut both ways.

One of the best things about sharing a common goal or vision is clear expectations. Expectations can be the most enabling or the most crippling factor in a relationship. When you have clear expectations, you can be on one accord, and when you are on one accord, you can be united. Expectations allow you to focus and channel your thinking, energy, and actions in the right way. Thus, expectations propel you toward your vision faster since you are acting and living in accordance with what you need to do to achieve your vision.

Expectations can have the opposite effect if they are out of sync with your partner or, even worse, unknown. When expectations are clear, it is easy to know when you are meeting expectations, exceeding expectations, or missing expectations. When expectations aren't voiced or known, you are acting with no idea about the impact your actions can have. How can your partner exceed your expectations, or even meet them, if they don't know what they are? You can't be upset with them for not bringing you flowers on Valentine's Day if they don't know that is what you expect. You can't be discouraged if they spend Saturday night with their friends instead of with you if you don't tell them you want Saturday night to be your date night. We know what some of you are thinking—they should just know that, but they don't. Nowhere in the definition of expectation is osmosis. Your partner only knows what you want when you tell them what you want, and that is how to best set expectations.

You cannot have two separate visions and thrive as a team. As someone once said, "Two visions mean division." Can you imagine how difficult it would be to be the non-politically aspiring partner in the Fosters' marriage and be a private person? It is critical that both couples are on the same accord. For some couples, this may mean that one partner is the leader that sets the vision and the other partner leads by executing their role with excellence.

Compromise is inevitable but shouldn't be so drastic that either partner feels undervalued or marginalized.

Goals are what you're going to do and by when.

To achieve a vision, a team must have objectives and/or goals. Objectives are the things we want to achieve. A mission, as discussed earlier, is a kind of objective, as it is focused on the primary way we will achieve our vision. Goals are an objective with more specificity, like a time period for completion or a metric for measurement. Given the vision of our three couples, let's see examples of goals they might have:

Couple	Goal
The Millers	Achieve a household income of $200,000 in the next ten years.
The Carters	Parent five kids in the next ten years.
The Fosters	Win our second election in the next ten years.

Strategy is how you will and how you won't.

Since there are many different ways you might achieve your goal, you use strategies to make choices and focus your actions. Strategies are the set of choices that we are going to make to reach our goals. It is just as much about what we are going to do as what we are not going to do. Here are strategies these couples might utilize to reach their goals (with alternative strategies in parentheses):

Couple	Strategy
The Millers	Work at the same company until we reach the executive level. (Go back to graduate school to qualify for a higher-paying job.)
The Carters	Add a new child to our family every three years. (Only grow family through adoption.)
The Fosters	Move through the state government system with a focus on Senate seats. (Excel in a business career and eventually enter government at the national level.)

Measured is as measured does.

Measures are an indication of progress toward the goals that you set. Let's see how these couples might measure how they are doing given their goals:

Couple	Measures
The Millers	Income level. Location of our residence.
The Carters	Number of children in our family. Size of our residence.
The Fosters	Name recognition in community. Length of our residency.

Write and revisit for accountability.

Your vision and strategic plan are not completely and truly built until you write them down on paper. Do you know any great teams that don't have a playbook?

While learning and alignment can come from strategic conversations about your relationship, documentation of plans demonstrates the commitment to them, allows for accountability, and is an easy reminder to what you agreed. It is also a great way to capture the history and growth of your relationship. We fondly look back on our five-year strategic plan that we made during our first year of marriage, marvel at where we were, and are proud that some things have changed (for the better) and that some things have stayed the same (for the better too).

Most companies revisit their strategic plan at least once a year. Companies spend up to six months in their strategic-planning process. We recommend revisiting your strategic plan at least twice a year or sooner, especially if any major life changes take place. From this plan can flow many other plans, such as budgets, career paths, travel calendars, and weekly activities. No matter what, it is important that both partners are aligned, willing, and able to be accountable and take a leadership role in achieving your shared vision. Make it fun; develop your plan at an annual retreat like executives do, with plenty of opportunities to work hard and play hard in the process.

The Bottom Line

- Build your vision together. It must be mutual and shared to work.
- Expectations can make or break your relationship. Make it easy on yourselves and communicate them early and often.
- Strategic planning can be a wonderful enabler of productivity in a marriage. It gets everyone on one accord. Remember, there is nothing you can't do if you are doing it together.
- Be accountable to your vision and plans. Write them down and revisit them regularly to stay on track.

Learn to Be Powerful

> I am always ready to learn although I do not always
> like being taught.
>
> —Winston Churchill

Let's face it—change is inevitable. Everything can and will change. The only way to stay current and relevant in life and in love is to adapt to change. That is why in every aspect of life, a commitment to learning is a competitive advantage. The business that commits to learning so they can adapt to changes in the marketplace will win. The business that refuses to learn will become extinct. To take advantage of change, one must learn to be flexible and welcome change. No matter how good or bad change feels, change always provides an opportunity to grow.

Perspective is a beautiful thing.

We think learning can act like both the sun and shade with regard to change. Like the sun, learning illuminates, allowing you to see things more clearly. It can also provide warmth and reassurance, as we know the sun will both rise and set every day. Learning can also bring shade and coverage, protecting you from overexposure to harmful things and shielding you from a negative perspective. So much of successful learning is all about having the right perspective and keeping a tight reign of control of that perspective. This means that you take an active role in what the business world calls controlling the narrative. You have a choice in every situation, especially when it comes to your relationship, to put everything in the proper and most appropriate perspective. We tested this concept against every marital challenge we could think of, and in each instance, we could imagine a positive outcome by controlling our perspective in the following areas:

- The facts—what is the truth?
- The learning—what can I take away from this that will help me grow?
- The context—what external factors are influential here?
- The future—how will I use this to live my life moving forward?

Our catchall is simply asking oneself, "What can I take away from this change to make me a better person and partner in the days to come?" This is a way to control your perspective and keep it healthy and forward-looking.

Learning creates leverage—in life and in love.

To truly be open to learning, partners must both accept three fundamental facts:

- You are both imperfect, will make mistakes, and are never finished growing.
- There is a clear difference between what your partner is able to do and what they are willing to do.
- You will both experience things, together or apart, that have the potential to bring significant change to your marriage.

Our focus on mutual self-discovery has led to an easier interpretation of each other's needs. Since we are mutually curious about each other, it makes us both feel important and interesting. It forces us to articulate our feelings, from the big stuff (like our ambitions, beliefs, values, and dreams) to the little stuff (like how we like our eggs cooked, where we like to sit in the movie theater, or if we really need to exchange gifts on our birthdays). It also forces us to be more introspective about whom we are becoming and how we are changing from the way we were before. As we are changing, we have to be vigilant in communicating how we are changing so our partner can understand, help, and champion those changes.

This is also very consistent with our earlier insights about building a vision. If things change, you may gain new perspective that might alter your strategic plan. Your partner needs to know this so you can both stay on track.

The following six concepts have accelerated learning in our relationship.

Acknowledge the difference between willing and able.

It is critical to know what your partner is able to do versus what they are willing to do. *Able* is physically, mentally, emotionally being able to do so, whereas *willing* means possessing the interest and desire to do so. Be aware of the trade-offs your partner is willing to make and not willing to make. How do you know? You ask.

Our advice? Know the difference, respect the difference, and keep searching for those things that aren't a willing-versus-able compromise. For us, Yahtzee needs to be played before 10:00 PM, and fifty degrees is the minimum temperature required for golf.

Turn nagging into navigation.

We don't bring up a problem to each other without simultaneously bringing up a solution. This works wonders in the workplace too. Bringing up a problem without a solution has a few typical labels: nagging, whining, and complaining. Bringing up a problem and a solution together has a few typical labels too: trying, problem solving, caring, peacemaking, and helping. It is like navigation. Navigators help the drivers get on and stay on the right path to reach their destination by providing the direction (or the solution) for where they need to go. Try it. The more often you do it, the more automatic it will be. If you don't have a solution, say so.

Show your partner that you made an effort to develop a solution.

Create playtime—play house, play fight, play everything.

This is one of our favorite tactics that we recommend to new couples we encounter. What's great is that no matter what stage you are in your relationship, you can try this too. The concept is simple: practice prepares for performance in the real situation, like the big game or the big meeting.

Before a big performance, performance artists do a dress rehearsal to practice what they will be performing to simulate what they will do. Fire drills simulate and prepare us for what to do if a fire breaks out. So, we play fight. We practice conflict when there is no conflict. We practice working our way out of indecision when there is no indecision. That way, when conflict arises, and it inevitably will, we are so much more comfortable and faithful that a solution is possible because we've had the conversation before. This also diffuses the drama that comes with conflict, like raised voices, funny looks, and huffing and puffing.

Early in our relationship, we practiced resolving conflicts that we understood to be typical of most relationships; so when conflicts arose, we were experienced at resolving them. Essentially, we would say to each other, "If this happened, how would you feel?" or "What do you believe about this?" In each case, we came back to "What if I disagree?" We talked through all the big stuff—money, chores, infidelity, raising kids, where to live, career trade-offs, etc.—when we were relaxed, carefree, and in great moods. Afterward, when conflicts arose, we were experienced at dealing with it in a constructive way. We believe that a big reason why fights get intense is the adrenaline rush of the moment. People get really excited and anxious when they don't know what is coming. Someone sneaking up on you will jolt your nerves much more than if you were told that someone will be walking in the door in two minutes, and they do. It is the same deal with conflict. If we've already discussed an issue beforehand, calmness is more likely than drama, certainty will replace surprise, and talking is traded for yelling. Ideally, the more issues you confront before they happen, the less chance that they will ever come up as issues.

When we were engaged to be married, we got a lot of advice regarding how all couples fight about money. So, over dinner one night, we just grilled each other about money. Questions we explored were the following: Are we going to combine accounts? Are you a spender or a saver? How much money should we save each month? What should we use credit for? How did your parents manage money? Do you want to do things the same or different from that? Who keeps the budget? Who opens the mail and bills? Who pays the bills? Who tracks the bills? If one of us doesn't work, how will we share money? Now, when those issues come up, we've already talked about them once before and know where each other stands. Drama averted.

Disarm with charm.

Despite all the play fighting and practice you can stand, you still have to learn how to have a productive discussion when conflict exists. We do a few things to disarm each other. One thing we do is give notice that a conflict might be coming, just like a meteorologist advising that storm might be in the forecast. We say to our partner, "I'm going to tell you something that you might not like. Ready?" We think that's only fair. If it looks like I'm going to hit you with a golf ball, I should at least yell "Fore!" If I'm going to cut a hundred-foot tree down, I should at least yell "Timber!" Giving some advance notice about the potential for a tough conversation ahead can only help.

A second thing that we do is take away all distractions and overemphasize giving each other our complete attention. We turn off the TV and/or stove. We pull the car over. We stare at each other (to see the attentiveness), hold hands (to feel the attentiveness), and talk in a quieter-than-normal voice (to require each other to work a little harder to listen to what is said).

Lastly, we close with some physical measure of mutual admiration, congratulations, or closure. What do teams do after a game? Shake hands. Doing something physical after a fight, like a high five, a hug, a pound, or a slap on the back, brings closure and says, "Nice job. That's over. We're moving on."

Get smart on what matters—them.

We know a lot about the things that interest us or are important to us, and that knowledge is called expertise. Given how important your partner is to you, shouldn't you be an expert on them? Some of you know more about the vital statistics and daily whereabouts of your favorite celebrity than you do your own partner, which is an imbalance in priorities. Gaining expertise on all aspects of your partner is of paramount importance. Tend to your flock. Golf your own ball. Where we come from, this idea is summed up by "mind your business."

Build a desire to be incurably curious about your partner. The more you know, the less you have to guess. The more you know, the more you can do to meet and even anticipate their needs. The more you know about them, the more you can help them be their best. Plus, you will feel better and more successful in your role as their partner too.

Accept help to see the blind spots.

One important concept for us is the blind spot. A blind spot is a realization or understanding about yourself that you either acknowledge as a weakness or are not aware of at all. This is the same concept as the blind spot present while driving a car. You may have visibility of that area behind you, but sometimes there is space that you cannot see—even though your perception of what you can see is a clear view. This is where your partner can be invaluable to you. Just like in a car, they may be able to see an area of potential risk or danger, based on low visibility you have versus the increased vantage point they might have. They know you so well and have been traveling life's journey with you such that they might be able to see your blind spots even if you can't. Sometimes, it is best to trust their view versus your own.

The Bottom Line

- Invest time to increase your knowledge of your partner.

- Learn how to constructively deal with the common challenges that every couple faces. Practice makes perfect.

- Your relationship will require study and constant examination as you and your partner change over time.

Execute for Excellence

Nothing will work unless you do.

—Maya Angelou

Awesome ideas and outstanding plans can never come to life without execution. You can't achieve anything—in business, in marriage, or life—if you are unable to execute. In your marriage, your level of execution is a direct result of your planning and your ability to work together. This is critically important because you can have all the potential for bliss in the world, but if you cannot work together, then it is all for naught. For us, working together is a simple, continuous, three-step process—say, do, and review.

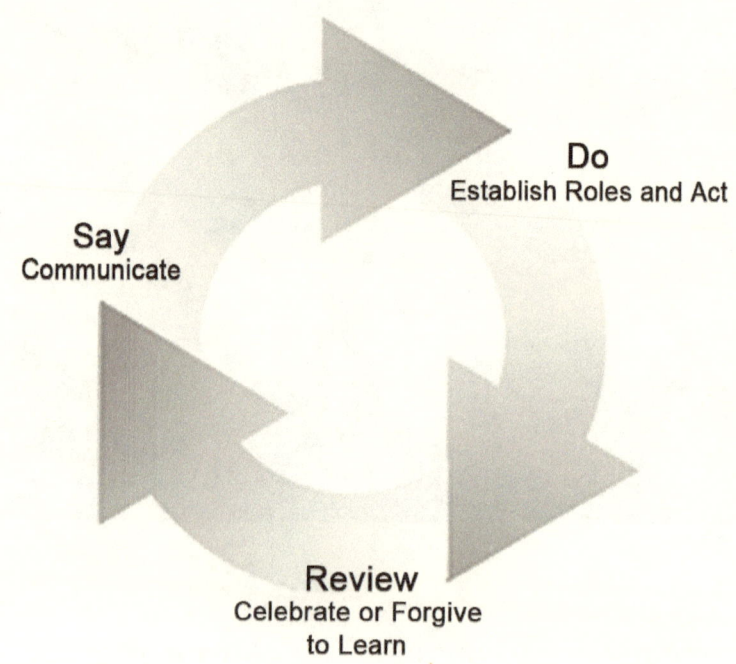

Say what you mean.

If you and your partner are going to work together, you have to be able to communicate with each other effectively.

The secret lies in your ability to share information in a way that the other person can receive it. You want your partner to not only see or hear what you are sharing, but you want them to also understand it. To learn what works best, you can study your partner as well as ask them how they want you to share information with them. You may find (or you may already know) what works for you may not work for them.

Edrienne and I have different preferences when it comes to answering questions about a situation. I have learned that Edrienne likes to hear the complete background and challenges of a situation before I ask her a question. This is how she likes to receive information in order to understand it and give her best response. I, on the other hand, am just the opposite. I like to hear the question first. This insight about each other has helped us both be better listeners and conversationalists—both with each other and with others.

Ineffective communication is often driven by laziness. Instead of trying to be understood and focusing on having a two-way conversation, sometimes we care more about being heard. The worst offense, however, is not giving your partner the same level of respect that you give to others. Would you raise your voice or point your finger at your boss, good friend, or even a casual acquaintance? We doubt it. Commit to talking to your partner in a way that is helpful, respectful, and gets through to them. More than anyone, they deserve the most respectful, patient, courteous, and caring level of communication you are capable of giving.

Do what you have to do.

All effective teams have defined roles. We have never seen a sales team where all members call on the same accounts in the same regions instead of dividing up territories. We have never seen a football team where all eleven players each try to hike, throw, catch, and run the ball. But we have seen quite a few couples who don't take the time to clearly define roles within their marriage.

Role definition allows a team to accomplish more by

- Leveraging each other's strengths,
- Dividing and conquering to provide coverage for all needs,
- Allowing people to lead and/or follow,
- Increasing productivity, and
- Creating shared responsibility.

To make roles stick, you must trust, be accountable, and be honest with your partner. Trust is important because to effectively separate tasks, you must be able to trust that your partner will do their part. You must do your part and be accountable for what you agreed to do. Honesty will help you not only commit to the right role for yourself, but will also help you keep expectations of what you can deliver in check.

When you put personal pride and ego aside, you can accept that there are things that your partner can do better or would rather do than you. For some couples, this is a hard concept to grasp, but for us, we use it to our advantage. We know that we have different strengths. Rather than insist that one of us always leads, we seek opportunities to maximize our individual talents and strengths. Not only does this allow us to be more efficient and accomplish more as a couple, but it also gives us opportunities to lead and shine within our marriage.

> *One of the best things that I could have done was to be honest with Wes about my lack of skill in cooking. Fortunately, Wes appreciates other things I do well and makes the choice to be with me regardless. In our relationship roles, we leverage strengths of mine, like organizing, budgeting, and planning. Thanks to Wes's willingness to accept me for who I am, I feel like I'm contributing to our relationship in a way that is meaningful, adequate, and fun.*

At the heart of execution is action. Actions are where the foundation you've set—your vision, plans, role definition, and expectations—all come to life. There are two levers you have to improve the effectiveness of your actions:

initiative and follow-through. Demonstrating initiative is acting independently of outside influence or control. Does your partner have to remind you to do the things that you are accountable for? If so, you might need to step up your level of initiative. Follow-through is pressing on in an activity until the activity is over. Do you have to be reminded to finish what you started? Do you do things halfway? If so, that might be indicative of challenges with follow-through. The good news is that excellence in both of these areas is fueled by your desire and ability to please and meet the needs of your partner. As that desire grows stronger in you, your propensity to act without outside influence improves. You two may find yourselves in a situation you have never seen before, but if you are well informed, you can anticipate your partner's needs and take the initiative to act and to follow-through.

Take the time to review.

A critical part of executing with excellence is taking the time to review how effectively you are working together. Inherent in this review is an assessment of previous actions that were aimed at achieving a certain goal or meeting a certain expectation, like fulfilling your household duties or keeping your established time commitments. These assessments provide yet another opportunity to learn about each other and yourself.

When expectations are met, celebrate that success with your partner. It is so easy to forget to acknowledge actions that meet expectations. Expectations are harder to meet than they are to miss. Years and years of met expectations without acknowledgment could lead to apathy. The best cure for apathy is appreciation. There is nothing like appreciation to build initiative and make someone want to do more of something. It is simple. Try the following: Thanks for working out with me. Thanks for dinner. Thanks for representing me well. Thanks for challenging me. Thanks for taking care of me. Thanks for going to work every day to support our family. Thank you for coming home early. Thanks for playing golf with me. Thanks for sticking to our budget. And then tell them why you are thankful. We doubt they will mind if you thank them every day for something.

In any long-term relationship, expectations will be missed. When expectations are not met by your partner, it is important to do the following two things in order to achieve a state of forgiveness. First, you should help your partner understand how they did not meet your expectations and the impact it had on you, be it hurt feelings or disappointment. Second, you should offer them a path to reconciliation. Let them know what they can do to curb your disappointment and rebuild your trust. Couples that are self-aware and work well together are very good at forgiveness because they know they are both imperfect people. They acknowledge and address issues, reconcile with each other, and move on.

The Bottom Line

- Continually say, do, and review to improve your ability to work together.
- Make the extra effort to effectively communicate with your partner.
- Establish and be accountable to your roles.
- Act with initiative and follow-through.
- Don't forget to celebrate and forgive.

Seek the Next Level

And let us consider one another

in order to stir up love and good works.

—Heb. 10:24

We constantly push and challenge each other because we want the best for each other and our marriage. We are each other's biggest fan and supporter as well as each other's toughest challenger and most honest critic. What else would you expect and want from your life partner and the person who knows you better than anyone else?

There is an art to the push.

Ephesians 4:15 reads, "But speaking the truth in love, may grow up in all things into Him who is the head—Christ." To push effectively, we must speak the truth and do so from a place of benevolence. Anyone who is committed to growth should agree. Unfortunately, many couples miss this opportunity to grow by only getting this partially right. Let's start with the first part.

"Speaking the truth" is so important. Way beyond the basic covenant of honesty and integrity that you have with your partner, it is one of the only ways to make dramatic improvements for the better in your lives together. To this end, we talk, talk, and talk some more. We talk about everything, as we believe that there is no such thing as overcommunication in a marriage. Sure, there can be overcommunication in one setting. It is really important to be open about what is going on in your mind so you can stay in sync with each other. Random stuff—no matter how corny or irrelevant—helps you get to know each other better. Tough stuff—no matter how difficult it might be to say—keeps things from festering, thickens bonds, and deepens trust. In either case, you may unlock opportunities or ideas that may change the game for the better for you both. Many CEOs work very hard to create a culture where people get used to sharing bad news. That way, everything is out in the open, and they can proactively address issues before they become problems.

The second part, "in love," implies the intent. You love your partner and intend to help your partner by telling them the truth. We all have a lot of commitments and responsibilities to think about and manage. Sometimes, we love our partner so much that the last thing we want to do is add to their already full plate by "speaking the truth" about something that really needs to be said. Avoiding confrontation with your partner can lead to acceptance and tolerance of things and behaviors that could be detrimental to the relationship.

To truly push and challenge yourselves effectively and yield new results, you must employ both parts well. We must confront our partners when necessary, but do it from a place of love and genuine care for them. We must focus on the objective of always trying to build them up and make them better and never trying to tear them down.

Wield the power of your words.

While "speaking the truth" is important, how you deliver the truth can be just as important as the truth itself. Sometimes, just your word choice or tone alone might imply that you are not speaking from a place of "love" even if you are. Sounds elementary, but never underestimate the power of your words. They can imprison just as easily as they can free. They can lift high and push low. Words can change someone's mood, someone's beliefs, or someone's life. Everything out of your mouth should be for the glory of God and the love of your partner. So wield the power of your words wisely.

It starts with you.

To be able to take your relationship to the next level, you must do your part by pushing and challenging yourself to be the best partner you can possibly be. We could spend so much time on this concept alone, but here are the highlights:

- Know yourself.
- Develop yourself.
- Strengthen yourself.

When we are weak, we are susceptible to influence, like a blade of grass in the wind. Deal with issues that are dragging you down—whether it is a person, a bad situation, or an unfortunate life event—and move forward. The stronger you are, the more you will have to offer your partnership.

Give your body, your mind, and your soul two things. First, give them attention. Stretch and push your body. Treat it well. Only put things in your body that will give you energy, a satiated feeling, and positively contribute to your health. Similarly, stretch, push, and stimulate your mind. Ideate, dream, and think about what could be. Cultivate your soul. Meditate, pray, and spend time getting in touch with your feelings. Stretch your senses and enjoy the world around you.

In conjunction with attention, you must also give your body, mind, and soul protection. We are very, very protective of ourselves, as we consider our minds and bodies our gifts to each other and the vessels that show the world who we are. So we protect ourselves from things that do not strengthen us. When we got engaged, there were relationships we ended. Why? We protect ourselves from potential negative influences and energy. There are places we don't go, things we don't do, and things we don't allow our eyes to see. We care too much about each other to treat ourselves any other way.

The Bottom Line

- Always push from a place of love to build up your partner, not to break them down.
- Focus on what you say and how you say it.
- Push yourself to be stronger to make your marriage stronger.

Parting Thoughts

All truths are easy to understand once they are discovered; the point is to discover them.

—Galileo

Nothing worth having is ever easy to acquire. You have to work to have the marriage that you want. By keeping God at the center of your marriage, committing to grow together, and being continually appreciative of the gift of marriage God has given you, the power of two will be yours to enjoy.

Index

www.ingramcontent.com/pod-product-compliance
Lightning Source LLC
Chambersburg PA
CBHW020347290526
45785CB00005B/2181